Red Has No Reason

poems by

JoAnne Growney

Plain View Press
P.O. 42255
Austin, TX 78704

plainviewpress.net
sb@plainviewpress.net
512-441-2452

Copyright © 2010 JoAnne Growney. All rights reserved under International and Pan-American Copyright Conventions. No part of this book may be reproduced or distributed in any form or by any means, or stored in a data base or retrieval system, without written permission from the author. All rights, including electronic, are reserved by the author and publisher.

ISBN: 978-1-935514-52-7
Library of Congress Number: 2010924971

Cover art by Florence Putterman.
(www.putterman.com)

Cover design by Susan Bright.

*Dedicated to the memory of
Amalie "Emmy" Noether (1882-1935):
the woman I followed into mathematics;
a poet of logical ideas.*

Acknowledgements

I am grateful to these magazines and anthologies in which versions of poems in *Red Has No Reason* have appeared:

"Keeping Watch" and "Write from the Beginning" in *Watershed*, January 2009; "Floating" and "A Taste of Mathematics" in *Strange Attractors: Poems of Love and Mathematics*, A K Peters, Ltd, 2008; "Mitigation of Toxins" in *Innisfree*, March 2007; "Not for Praise" in *Focus*, October, 2006; "The April Lover" in *Divided City*, Autumn 2006; "Horizon" in *Poet Lore*, Spring / Summer 2006; "How Did It Come to This?" in *Innisfree 2*, Spring 2006, and in *Byline*, 2004; "Angles of Light" and "Call Me Ramona" in *Palpable Clock*, University of Scranton Press, 2004; "A Woman Is a Gallery She Can't Stop to View" in *BigCityLit*, December 2003; "Pages of Unsaid Words" in *Out of Line*, 2003; "Fear" in *Hanging Loose 81*, Fall 2002; "Stress Remedy" in *Rattapallax 7*, Spring 2002; "View From the Moon" in *Carver*, Spring 2002; "Today at the Grocery Store I Met the Man I Loved" in *Sou'wester*, Spring 1999; "Stories" in *Explorations*, 1998; "Running" in *Pennsylvania English*, Fall 1998; "Things to Count On" in *Carver*, Spring 1998;"Conditionals" in *Yarrow*, Fall/Winter 1997-98; "Present Tense" in *Ginger Hill*, Spring 1997; "Carry a Stone" in *Yarrow*, Fall/Winter 1996-97; "Snowbound" in *Four Quarters*, Spring 1995.

Versions of "Butterfly Proposal," "Can a Mathematician See Red?" "Conditionals," "Small Squares," "The Bear Cave," "Things to Count On," "The Strong Flavor of Mathematics" and "Time" have appeared in a chapbook of mathematical poems, *My Dance is Mathematics*, Paper Kite Press, 2006; and versions of the poems in section 2 (memory) appear in a chapbook, *Angles of Light*, Finishing Line Press, October, 2009.

Contents: Red Has No Reason

1 (attention)

How Did It Come to This?	9
Beyond Habits	10
Trompe L'oeil	11
Pandemonium	12
Exercise	13
Clarification	14
The Suicide Mission	16
Department Store	17
The Bear Cave	18

2 (memory)

Write From the Beginning	21
24 / 7 Exhibition	22
Horizon	23
More Than Granaries Can Hold	24
Present Tense	25
Stories	26
Symmetry	27
Carry a Stone	29
Things to Count On	30
Can a Mathematician See Red?	31
Keeping Watch	32
Night Sky	33
View from the Moon	34
Today at the Grocery Store I Met the Man I Loved	35
Resisting Mourning	36
Susquehanna Winter	37
Snowbound	38
Angles of Light	39

3 (resistance)

Pages of Unsaid Words	45
On Deaf Ears	46
Filling the Vacuum	47
Change	48
Leaning Left Is Right	49
Not for Praise	50
A Taste of Mathematics	51
14 Syllables	52
Some Squares	53
Mitigation of Toxins	55

4 (complexity)

Turns	59
Time	60
Like a Cat	61
Fear	62
The April Lover	63
12 Syllables	65
Call Me Ramona	66
Butterfly Proposal	67
Conditionals	68
Stress Remedy	69
I Don't Know Much about Gods	70
Running	71
A Woman Is a Gallery She Can't Stop to View	72
The End Begins with a Word	74
April	75
Aurora Borealis	76

Notes	77
About the Author	79

1
(attention)

How Did It Come to This?

Prints on exhibit walls—
notions of a bull by Picasso,
whose clear eye directed a deft hand.
Careful likeness becomes surreal
design then sketch
and in the end
a few fine lines.
Poems also we make
by erasing.

Beyond Habits

Camouflaged in shades of shadow,
magicians dwell where strangeness
is so usual nothing's strange.
Intent approaches, then turns to slip
behind the habits that perfect
a skill. Never mistake magic
for art—here are no vagaries:
magicians train as pole-vaulters do—
tedious, lonely practice
broken by a moment's flight.

Trompe L'oeil

September afternoon,
a lawn-chair woman lazes
with a Sunday paper spread.
Squirrels drop from hemlocks
to her tin garage roof.

Next door's neighbor
hammers one-two-THREE,
one-two-THREE, ONE, ONE.
Between his blows dogs bark,
a lawnmower whirrs.

Scavengers in last night's tuxedos find
pencils in sidewalk cracks. From a kitchen,
a short-shorts daughter calls,
why can't I use the dishwasher?
The woman sees tigers

pacing in zoos, spraying
and spraying again the walls
so rivals don't come near.
She peels a cabbage leaf by leaf,
accepts the core in half-chewed bites

that burn but have no taste.
Details mask control as in
a circus clown's careful plan.
What secret does this canvas
illuminate?

Pandemonium

some gallery visitors find fiery hell
in russet swirls but I see dust near Kokomo
where gardens highways tombstones glare
red clouds pervade parched August air
hang dance in sunbeams and disappear

mammals wear features human faces blur
brittle glacial blue no world ends
in ice instead of hell or paradise a circus tent
pitched on dusty stubble empty town
songless birds and elephants slow down

shadow women cling to edges never know
poets in their El Dorado circus clowning
high trapezes open cages bareback lust
elephants remember perfect nonsense
searching women's faces birds fall into dust

Exercise

The warm-up track for harness-racers
is my favorite place to jog—
my spine and knees and ankles like the soft
landings of my sneakers on loose sand
and, though I'm regularly passed,
I'm saluted with sulky drivers' nods
and whinnies from the sturdy Standard-breds—
these horses lift my spirits and, at last,

my legs find steady pace, my chestnut mane
rises and floats. My gallop lifts me beyond
the turn of track, across the field, past traffic.
I don't hear auto horns, don't feel the stares
of bystanders. I rise to where words draft
themselves into swinging, ringing bells.

Clarification

1

Old women can't be born, can't
enter mother's womb. Rebirth
is water, spirit. The wind sings distant.
What's its name? Where's its home?

2

It's time for cleansing. I start at night and go
till noon. Blank walls all dark at first
but I find chalk—small polyhedral chunks
from blackboard trays—and brightly scrawl.

First I write myself: my curls, the accident
that left my forehead scar, my first book
learned by heart—too hot, too cold, too small,
just right. Then the pet orphan lamb
soon strong enough to jerk his bottle from my hand,
the mother who loved me with an iron hand, the father
who gave his hand instead of words, the sister
whose ill health gave her the upper hand.

Dust-white soft limestone from fossil shells—
packed cylinders of foraminifers now press
the hum of mind to words—between the lines
tell more, explain—help me forgive
my father dying, leaving me to wear
my mother—tight hat lastingly impressed—
noisy fearful rigid balance: novel-sermon,
kiss-equation, college-kitchen, bye-bye-love.

I write and write to cover walls
with white chalk crumbs—a good day ends.
Resting, I think of Tom, then inside every "o"
I squeeze his name—not the disappointment
but the boy who raced me on his bike.

3

pen-strokes on paper,
mirrored reflection,
footprints in mud,
shadow on sidewalk,
lipstick on glass,
angel in snow.

4

Didn't imagine
rebirth this way:
whitewash
the walls!
Okay.

5

You can get used to things, slide into routines, bury the wish to wake up new in the old place glowing with pristine cells that flex open with wonder and fear. Right now, this is different—there's been a death, the past is penned away. You have written the walls white, pressed detail inside event until it's all one piece and deserves to be called a blank slate—you've sent things out of your mind, found their ends.

6

After she made light, she divided it into darkness. She invented dials and flowering and seasons that measure night. She tamed a dog to walk beside and listen. She fitted her body with a womb and flowing blood.

7

Night ghosts linger above the pines,
their lamps trembling red and green.
Dogs bark at white peaks
where spirits call back time.

The Suicide Mission

        There is no stronger urge
than species' drives to breed their kind.
        Chinook salmon
challenge current, surge upstream to spawn.
        In this foreign water
the Chinook male starves into monster—
        his eyes sink back,
his upper jaw curves downward like a hook,
        dog-teeth extend :
bright magnificence fades to spotted martyr.

Department Store

The perfume clerk eats sausage gravy
on biscuits for breakfast. At forty
she abandoned her daughter—brushed
her teeth and left—suitcase in hand,
paisley handbag over her shoulder.

TV news gives to horror free gift-wrap.
Before the drowning Susan took off
their socks and shoes. She begged
for the electric chair—promised if
she had more children she'd kill them too.

Nothing frightens me except a dead child.
Sell me a necklace to brighten my old dress.
While I complain of sales tax tell me stories
of reincarnation. Tell me how to find him
when the corpse becomes somebody else.

The shoe salesman puzzles a question, *are you
thinking better than me?* I consider. While he
ties knots and speaks in a low voice, I wonder
if he has made children with anyone. I want
to grow tulips that flame at one another.

The Bear Cave

Twenty-five years ago at Chiscau, marble quarry workers discovered, trapped by an earthquake in a wondrous, enormous cave, bones of one hundred and ninety bears, *Ursus spelaeus* (now extinct). Cold rooms of cathedral splendor now render tourists breathless while the insistent drip of water counts the minutes. There is no safe place.

2
(memory)

Write from the Beginning

for Adda Isabel Black Simpson Stephens (1912-2007)

Write about it, they said,
without using the word.

I could not and then,
suddenly, she was there—
my mother, who cries
when she's happy, who talks fast
when she's tired, who acts silly
when she's sad. Yes, I said,
I'll tell of birth, the baby
bloody new into the world,
ready for all things, started
on a journey that will end.

24/7 Exhibition

The racks of candy bars arrest me:
I squint at deep displays of wrappers—
extravagantly red—and watch girls
leave this shop for school with pockets full
of shiny paper, milk chocolate and crunch.
I swallow color and crave a taste
of sweetened childhood hours:
moments free of purpose—never counting
pennies or Necco wafers.

Horizon

All was heaven, once, and seamless—
no dark to change shine into glare,
no clouds to fear.

None were wise or ignorant, no secrets
whispered in the breeze — there were
no better days.

Apples were mere apples, mix of tart and sweet.
Silent snakes ate insects, kept their earthbound place.
Opposites had not

declared themselves: delight and sadness,
fear and comfort blended, waiting for the seeker
to awake — to attend

the dying of the brightest star,
halving of the mind by the horizon
drawn near.

Divided
into complexity,
Eden disappears.

More Than Granaries Can Hold

for George Fulton Simpson (1906-1950)

He won't plant corn until the dogwoods bloom;
when thunder rolls, I hear him call the cows;
we don't make hay when circles ring the moon;
we snack on windfall apples—cut the bruises out.
Brave with him, I jump the pasture brook;
his hand steadies my wobbles on a bike.
Pressed side by side, we read *The Jungle Book*—
not yet, it's not yet time for turning out the light!

His sudden death has made me fear
good things—my heart is trapped
in that summer when wheat fields give more
than granaries can hold. Tapping a foot he claps
as I do a slipping two-step through the grain
spilled in abundance on our barn floor.

Present Tense

The cold moon made weird trees of corn shocks that leaned together against the winter. Every farmer but my father used a corn picker that left the stalks alone. My family's history is not the norm. We rushed ahead of progress or missed it, quoted when others improvised, weighed pros and cons although predestined, kept daybooks as if minutes matter.

My mother is a terrifying
woman. She eats anything.
I dreamed when the sun rose
she'd be a brick wall.

She is.

Stories

I'm stronger than my mother. I can shove her aside,
    beat her, burn a print of my hand on her behind.
        It's not too late to have a happy childhood —

to move from loneliness into a town house,
    to choose the bedroom with a note on the closet wall:
        We liked living here, hope you will too.

My life disconnected me. October, tenth grade —
    no time to change clothes after milking —
        at the football dance, my shoes carried manure.

Thirst for milk turns into new addictions — appetites
    for chocolate and intercourse, urgency to choose a time to die.
        See that the window's not centered between the cabinets.

Father's farm routines made plain, *Good habits*
    are good friends. I know, too, that whiskey is consolation,
        cigarettes are company — *bad* habits also are friends.

To brighten myself I bought red shoes. I wore them
    three times, and they were only shoes.
        Habits become ends.

Symmetry

After my father died, my mother
loved God and Esther Williams.
Nine years old—and oldest—I was
her right-hand helper; she took me
to the movies when she went.

Million Dollar Mermaid,
Neptune's Daughter,
Thrill of a Romance,
Easy to Love,
Dangerous When Wet.

Circles of swimmers
arch outward from centers,
gently blooming lilies,
supple bodies matched
in perfect timing.

Seated in the theater I watched
my mother dive without a splash,
go deep to glide, turn, and rise;
embraced by warm blue water,
her heavy grief transmogrified.

◯

Years later, the synchronized swimmers
come back to mind as my daughter and I stroll
cherry blossom weekend at the National Mall.
We watch six women draw their angelfish
up from the lawn. The kites shoot high

continued....

in one straight line, then dip and swoop,
split in pairs to left and right, make loops,
weave between each other
like the fingers of two hands,
pause and hover near the ground.

These kites glide from the women's arms
like graceful dancing daughters—
easy in obedience
to tugging strings.
And sometimes a kite falters.

Carry a Stone

for Anna Maria Wachob Black (1869-1957)

Bring your grandmother back with a story. Dream a story, dream it as you tell it, gathering others to enter the dream. Make the dead say, *Here are the raisin cookies I baked for you. Get out the checkers and let's have a game.*

Grandma taught me to bake bread. *Do it without thinking,* she said. *Punch and pull, let your mind make music, run, spend. Salt the dough with sweat from your palm. Don't be tight with butter. Don't mix too much.*

Three dresses are enough, she said — *two everyday, one dress-up. Get rid of things or spend your whole life tidying up. Polish your chair daily with a woolen cloth; the wood will soon be velvet. To improve the world, carry a stone to the top of the mountain.*

Concealing is the greatest art. Pretend to be free.

If I go in the car today, I may die. But today is a good day to die. Grandma said, *Death is like being in a book on a library shelf that nobody's reading.* I don't think so. Death is not finishing the book. You are most beautiful before you die. That is the story of my grandmother.

Things to Count On

I want to say how beautiful it was — but it was not. Each animal, each shed, each acre was useful; we kept them with good care and counted them, counted on them. One hundred forty acres, seven sheds. A white frame house, eight tall rooms and bath, a cellar with a dozen shelves for canned goods and four lines for laundry, a truck room for junk. We five in three bedrooms, four beds. One extra room for guests — my aunts. Our dining room with seven doors plus closets. A shed beside the corn crib with space for three wagons and a Plymouth. The barn with two mows for hay, a third for straw, a granary, a bathtub for livestock drinking, and six private stalls. Nine cows with two for milking, which I did. In seven days no minutes to be happy, no hours to be sad — not even when my father died. My mother's a good woman, worth three good women. For sixty years everyone has thought so, and more than a hundred have said. I've stopped counting.

Can a Mathematician See Red?

Consider the sphere —
a hollow rounded layer
whose points seen outside
are the very same points
insiders see.

If red paint spills
all over the outside,
is the inside red?

The mathematician says, *No,
the layer of paint
forms a new sphere
that is outside the outside
and not a bit inside.*

A mathematician
sees the world
as she defines it.

A poet
sees red
inside.

Keeping Watch

I clasp her hand but keep my thoughts aloof.
She speaks from time to time with practiced cheer—
never one to detail wounds, she nonetheless alludes
to pain much more than any one can bear
but bearable because her Christian Faith
holds Paradise against my dark resistance
to believe in Hell or Christ. Daily she's prayed
for me and warned me, persistent and intense—

she will save me yet. Though we sit silent, I play
her proselytizing voice against my inner ear
and resolve to make my own end free
of straining to make others live for me.
I watch for signals. *Anticipating Evil
helps it happen*, I tell her. This much I believe.

Night Sky

Tall in my backyard, a pine
reaches to the handle
of the Big Dipper.
I look again—connection's gone—
behind the silhouette of pine
random unnamed stars.

View from the Moon

Forget pollution, quake, and flood. One word,
in answer to a different question
than he meant to ask her, starts the fall
of meanings, the cascade to disaster.

Today at the Grocery Store I Met the Man I Loved

The frenzy of desire is absent now.
His words keep their distance like a radio voice.
Sparrows have returned to nest in corners of the porch,

and my body doesn't melt to his in any dream.

Daisies again bloom beside the fence,
and starlings fill trees with their chatter.
I mow the lawn and cut the honeysuckle back

and discover that nothing is the matter.

In the grocery aisle, we spoke of the weather
in our separate parts. Floods and storms
have abated. Nothing separates our hearts.

Resisting Mourning

Can't sleep. I reread your letter, hold
your photograph, wrinkle a smile, tremble
as I conjure the lips behind your moustache,
your air of discontent. You are

a rubber band about my wrist, reminder
that chords need silence, bent backs beg
their loads to bear. Make a phone call. Tell me

about the maple tree in your back yard—
does it still annoy you as, with great green fists,
it breezily resists the mourning doves.

Susquehanna Winter

Not all frogs are princes—still, I know a few
with royal lineage, and I can fight
the gloom of a December afternoon
remembering them. Long hours I sit and write

while winter holds our valley by the throat—
I try to shape words into a bright affair
that hugs more warmly than my long red coat
and curves closer than my leather chair.

My son suggests I quit these fantasies and get
a dog. Not now. I'm done with mothering.
I'll build new worlds with strings of alphabet—
then, after a dance with words, the rush of spring

will spread a quilt of violets beneath the cottonwood
and waken frogs to serenade from deep soft mud.

Snowbound

Snowbound is that other world
in which no schedules sit
and no ambitions flare
to interrupt the bluest sky
and whitest field
and coldest air.

Angles of Light

1

Conversation on the ferry turns to pink flamingos
that perch in Sitka spruce and draw tourists
to ask whether photos make plastic birds look real.

2

Seals bark greetings, ravens bless
our chimneys, mountains applaud.
Alaska catches us between
Eden's delight and the nonsense
of Utopia—dazzled, we enter
life's bargains unknowing—
become wolves, mosquitoes, bears.

3

This place makes my heart turn corners, learn
to trust the fierce geometry of angles, submit
to the care of rivers and peaks, allow
geography to bend, tear, reform.
My spirits ignite, my blood rushes
dark as mountain streams on the steep north face.
It costs my life to belong here
where December is dim, the light
acutest at its vanishing. Compressed
distance. Bronze snow heaped
on high horizons. The avalanche comes
when snow hangs heavier than the angle
of the mountain. June days so long
they forbid the aurora. Warmth
when rays escape the angle of the mountain—
the mountain closest in morning, the mountain
that exalts a man but makes his house small.

continued....

4

Three times the size of Texas,
Alaska—with fewer living species
and fewer miles of paved roads
than Rhode Island.

5

A moose needs swamp and willow,
a bear needs square miles,
the aurora needs a sky that's dark.

6

In his saloon, with a high-priced woman on each arm,
Jefferson Smith slips twenties inside wrappers of two
of his five-cent bars of soap—then, he pays sidekicks
to find the planted bills and boast of their good luck
to a full room of whiskied prospectors—gold rushers
itching for fortune's turn. Smith then offers to sell—
for a dollar—each of his lucky bars.

This was 1898—a small bar of soap, a great big dollar!
The false front of Soapy Smith's establishment
still stands in Skagway where it draws cruise ships of tourists
who smile during stories of swindles and sigh over men
who made laws against prostitution while they demanded it.

7

Back East, people choose whether
to live on a high floor or below,
to eat Turkish or Thai,
to shop at dollar stores or boutiques,
to go acrosstown or downtown
by taxi or bus,
to see a play or a film,
which bridge to cross.

Here the sunrise chooses
and the wind.
The mountains choose,
and the eagles.
The whales choose
and the salmon
and the stream.
The rainy mist chooses,
and distance decides,
and time is irrelevant,
and—if you want to stay—
you accept the idea of order
in Skagway. If you stay
you turn corners, bend angles,
give up doubt,
plant flamingos.

3
(resistance)

Pages of Unsaid Words

Three-quarter, five-quarter, eight-quarter inches—
black spring clamps sit in my desk drawer
waiting for sheets of words.

Triangle tunnels with steel, keyhole handles
anchor twenty pages or two hundred
with a squeeze that hurts the hand.

In Nanjing imprisoned women assemble
without wages three thousand clamps per day.
Dissidents and prostitutes attach stiff handles

and bleed.

On Deaf Ears

A group of teens
stretch with excitement,
watch for the downbeat
and begin—deaf singers
radiant as if they hear
the Bach they sing.
I hang on every syllable
as early notes that quaver
swell into cacophony.
                Oh! Swans!

Filling the Vacuum

In 1973
Billie Jean beat Bobby,
and abortion
became legal.

          O

My high school physics teacher
liked trick questions—
he claimed embarrassment
would help us to remember.

From "What's inside a tennis ball?"
he wanted "Nothing" so he could
laugh and say "There's air."
Nothing is a vacuum —

the ball implodes,
sucked to its center
like dust into a Hoover—
touted as a time-saving

invention, but women
know it raised only
our standards for clean.
Vacuuming a fetus

from its womb is an ounce
of prevention. Unwanted children
quit school before physics,
are twice as likely to be bad.

Change

Indians discourage it; tourists do it anyway—
give coins to a beggar, to the five who tag along.
Find more rupees for the tiny woman
pinching her baby to cry as she seizes your arm.

Friends advise: tomorrow, leave the Good Luck
Fast Food Vegetarian Restaurant by another door.
Walk the longer route to the grocery store.
Protect yourself. Hide fear. Eyes front. Ignore.

○

Is anyone unselfish? I consider Agnes—
that daughter of Albania who became Teresa
and gave herself to India. Charity is not
enough to make you beautiful. Colonists
grow ugly giving what hurts.

○

Returned from travels, are you different—
does understanding alter your view?

When beggars ask for change,
what do you do?

Leaning Left Is Right

Right there
on 8th Avenue,
her left arm stretches long
with grocery bags. Though she supposes
the strain draws her left,
we behind see her spine
curled right.

Not for Praise

The gravity of the universe
needs dark matter;
each of our choices
blocks out another:
graciousness takes time
away from mathematics.

Labyrinthine thoughts
mature in isolation—
genius slips if socialized:
Perelman refused the prize.

A Taste of Mathematics

A mathematician left the convention
focused on 9, the digit that sits
in the billionth decimal place of pi,
ratio of circumference to width
of the yellow circle that parted the clouds
as she strolled down Commerce Street
to the Rio Rio Café for lunch and a beer.

On fire with jalapeños
she went shopping
for a souvenir.
She bought earrings —
red-red plastic peppers
with green stems.

She said, "Hot peppers
are like mathematics —
with strong flavor
that takes over
what they enter."

14 Syllables

A hen lays eggs
one by one;
the way you
count life
is life.

Some Squares

Each of these stanzas is square—the number of syllables per line is the same as the number of lines.

> Mock feelings
> serve as well
> as true ones.

> Her lover left.
> She's in deep gloom.
> What she'd offered
> is now her own.

> When lovers leave,
> avoid laments—
> grab a cactus;
> new pain forgets.

continued....

All over the world
fashionable shoes—
trendy, hazardous,
uncomfortable —
keep women in place.

More than the rapist, fear
the district attorney,
smiling for the camera,
saying that thirty-six
sex crimes per year is a
manageable number.

Give up despair, let go self-love
that sees your heartache past repair,
ignoring friends as if not there,
turned in to shelter gloom and sear
your wounds, keeping them ragged, bare.
Examine choices—accept care
and empathy—a hand, an ear,
a voice—to soften the madness.

Mitigation of Toxins

A stand of poplars is a self-assembling
solar-powered pump-and-treat
ground-water protection system.
Brake ferns filter arsenic from soil;
Indian mustard drinks up lead.
Sunflowers shrink strontium levels.

    An uncommon man, an occasional woman,
    buffer the malice of others, keep
    the rest of us from tilting the world.

Phytostablization,
phytoextraction,
rhizofiltration,

    civilization.

4

(complexity)

Turns

When you enter a room wearing the amber ring,
you own the room, its tunes, its lights.
You could center the universe but you turn
and gather darkness; amber turns to lavender.

Time

I

The clock goes round —
showing time's a circle
rather than a line.
Each year's return to spring
swirls time on time.

II

Time's not
        as Newton said —
                the same for all —
for I
        am punctual,
                and you are late.
You waste
        the savings
                I spend on you.

III

Six o'clock does not exist, but at seven
she answers your knock, elegantly dressed
for the nineteen-jewel evening you've planned.

IV

At my time's end I want to rust away
like the graceful iron gate that wore jack-o-lanterns
in October, swung the lions of March winds,
struck the backsides of generations of women
bringing groceries to the kitchen door.

Like a Cat

Today I'm feeling like a cat but not
at all as Kipling said: *to cats all places
are alike.* I favor corners—hide my back
from wide expanse of gaping sky, appreciate
when trees ensnare my fleeting thoughts,
and narrow passages confine
my side-to-side meanderings on springy sod
that grounds me soft but not to stay.

The sky's a creature as alive as rocks
but not as warm—a wonder incompletely known
until it's time to leave. Cats sit composedly
and watch as dogs chase turning wheels, biting spin
as if they might roll distance into circles—
infinite turned finite—subtle, catlike trick.

Fear

Grandfather feared nothing on this earth
but doing wrong. Quick success got my life
off on the wrong foot. One of three antelopes
skimming across the rough terrain,
I never wished for others to falter.

I fear everything, reject bravery
for pleasantry. Grandfather's legacy a bomb,
terminally lit. I find shapes in the clouds
that pursue me, hide messages in things I don't say.
Did the world tilt or did it fail to tilt?

A traveler pays the plane fare, the hotel —
acts as if he owns the country. Experts
yield to those who know little. Or nothing.
It's possible I'll go on forever,
turning prayers into disappointments.

I ask God to show both hands at the same time,
want my silence to be a voice in the parallel world.
Hiding in a dark room, grateful to know so little
in advance. Merriment dangles from terror.
I'm all fingers; my eyes don't understand.

The April Lover

When he takes her
she makes her thighs respond,
lets her neck be stiff. She fixes

her eyes on the horizon, draws in and is
transported: her feet on matted grasses
sink to wet cold swamp.

If she wears shoes
they fill with water,
if her skirt is short

the brambles
scratch her legs,
if she bleeds

she doesn't feel
the blood's warm trickle,
if a dog

sniffs her crotch
she doesn't stoop
to stop it.

When the frenzy finishes
she'll fix her face, her hair,
pull in her chin,

offer squeezes of the hand,
reclaim herself with fists of chocolate,
inspect her life—zoom out and in.

Something should be broken,
but breaking necks
doesn't make them pliant.

Postures chosen early
are most difficult
to bend—

liars make good
lovers, committed
to pretend.

12 Syllables

Truth keep you distant.
Move closer and
lie to me.

Call Me Ramona

I am wise with clear sight or I'm the old one
        out to lunch in the park who takes off everything
but a bikini and socks. I close my eyes

and arrange the living room, moving the sofa
        a quarter turn. My dream loses a son
from the grocery store aisle to the circus

where elephants want someone to remember.
        Some thoughts have glue on them.
My mother packed my head full of underwear

labeled *virgin cotton*. I need a sound-track
        with red music that dances. Give me
a new, exotic name.

Butterfly Proposal

The future looks sad and scares you.
Don't let forebodings hush the echoes
of old voices—we need the past to build
high spirits. I'll write you
into a poem.

A butterfly on your hand proposes life—
a promise drawn at the intersection
of Broadway and Euclid, a fortunate convergence
that counters disillusion. Butterflies
are transient, illogical

while you wear every sort of rule
impalpable and tight. You shrink from praise
and flounder in the caramel of fear's sweet heat.
Your moth-mind skitters everywhere;
your deeds all are polite.

Twist your finger with rubber bands:
the throb will keep you sane. You don't
have to fix each broken thing. Adjust your ears;
hear slowly. Into the pauses,
understanding.

Conditionals

If you take a rose with petals curled
and put it in a vase beside the clock
that has no hands, someone you thought
was lost returns for morning tea.

If you push hard against your belly wall
and square your shoulders while no one
watches from the pines, you hear
your sister's whisper in distant highway noise.

If you slowly peel an orange after noon
and pluck tomatoes by the quarter moon,
you see beyond obsession to details.

If you walk the river's edge to pick up stones
and pile them to mark a place, tomorrow's dawn
shines bright upon your broken fingernails.

Stress Remedy

From the barn
bring the cow
to your living room rug.
Sleep
when the cow sleeps.

On your porch
watch the ant
do a task seven times.
Quit
before the ant quits.

Walk out
to the field
where wild mustard waves.
Spend
that gold right away.

I Don't Know Much about Gods

but they don't live in houses brightly painted
on narrow streets in small towns and don't
celebrate the ordinary as I do and my friends.

I doubt paradise. I see mostly what is small
and not too far away, dislike to start
new things, will build on old foundations.

No river runs in me, no sea surrounds.
My corner is a tidy garden plot.
I plant and nourish, pick the crop —

with care I cook, enjoy my fare, wash up,
and sleep to rise another day. Gods should
introduce themselves to girls like me.

Running

Response to "The Waking" by Theodore Roethke (1907-1963)

My sleep is brief. I rise to run again,
to flee the doubts that catch me when I'm still.
I live by going faster than I can.

I feel by doing. What's to understand?
I eat and drink and never have my fill.
My sleep is brief. I rise to run again.

I'm useful and adored. Supporters throw grand
parties in my honor, courting my good will.
I live by stepping higher than I can.

Restless at night, I reach and find a hand
to hold and squeeze, to drop with guilt —
after brief bothered sleep, I rise and run again.

I lack companions. Friendship's madly bland,
and no one keeps my pace in search of thrill.
I live by going faster than I can.

Motion holds me sane and so I run,
but the pace that keeps me lucid also kills.
My sleep is brief. I rise to run again.
I live by going faster than I can.

A Woman Is a Gallery She Can't Stop to View

I

One summer evening in the eighties—
an interview with Jackie O.
>What's your greatest achievement?
>>*I'm proud that I stayed sane.*
>What lies in your future?
>>*To learn how others see me.*

II

So, it's come to this. Sitting under a tree
in a state park in Oklahoma,
I find a seashell, pick it up
and hear a voice, *You are just like me.*

III

Everyone's met someone from out of town
who says, *My friend X in Baltimore
is just like you. Same hair, voice, and posture.
Even your gestures are the same.*

I want to meet my double, to ask her,
*Does your body hum beneath your thoughts?
Am I an easy imitation?
What's the cost of being me?*

IV

At family reunions, my uncle shows old films.
Restless me before the camera, darting, stopping.
Young, natural — more lovely than she knew —
but what's the use to know her since she's gone.

My mother made much of helpful little girls.
Praise still persuades me; I work hard
for words withheld. On the road from my house
to hers, a truck covers me with shadow.

V

The rim of darkness against sunlight
reminds me how things disclose at borders
with their opposites. I weave a blanket of words.
Prepared for everything. Unknown.

The End Begins with a Word

Startled Monday
      leaves dark warmth
      for words and willfulness,
      praise and praise withheld.

Tuesday links hands,
      learns routines,
      exchanges milk for chocolate,
      sees limits, thinks to fly.

Dressed to kill,
      Wednesday's earthquake
      splits a jasmine cloud
      into anxiety, tedium, upward mobility.

Thursday tries compromise.

Looking back, Friday falters,
      sees the edge—
      considers eternity, escape—
      saves a recipe, comes to a fence.

Saturday steams asparagus,
      weaves a crown of clover blossoms,
      wants to remembers something,

agrees to Sunday.

April

A woodpecker drums indigo into the poet's blue days. As she pens monsters, the bird taps. Reluctant, she rises and moves in slow green steps. Yellow with doubt she tracks the bird down streets of violet promises. Confetti gusts lift coats. Orange smiles erase objection to squirrels crunching birdseed — their plunder does no harm now when snow is gone. In the dollar store, she buys toilet paper. Her pain is white and ordinary and may be pushed away. She soon will yield to the rainbow's red ending.

Aurora Borealis

As there is no purpose for violet,
    there's no purpose for purpose.
As there's no order for orange,
    no order exists.
As green escapes gravity
    and indigo invites inertia,
    as blue begs argument
    and yellow fails to yield,
As red has no reason,
    reason is repealed.

Notes

1. Page 12—"Pandemonium" was inspired by "Blue Ladies and Elephants," a painting by Florence Putterman (www.putterman.com) that serves as the cover for this book.

2. Page 23, "Horizon"—The phrase, "halving of the mind by the horizon," adapts a line by Derek Walcott in "Names."

3. Page 27, "Symmetry"—The five phrases of stanza two name films in which Esther Williams starred.

4. Page 46, "On Deaf Ears"—This event that led to this poem are described in a *Washington Post* story by Blake Glopnik, May 28, 2006 and in a video by Artur Zmijewski, "Singing Lesson 2."

5. Page 50, "Not for Praise"—In August 2006 a Russian mathematician, Grigory Perelman, was selected for honor with the award of a Fields Medal for his proof of the century-old Poincaré conjecture. Perelman did not accept this award.

6. Page 51, "A Taste of Mathematics"—Announcement of the billionth decimal digit of π was made at the annual Joint Mathematics Meetings in San Antonio in January, 1993. Since then π has been calculated to more than a trillion digits.

7. Page 70, "I Don't Know Much about Gods"—This poem was prompted by "The Dry Salvages" by T S Eliot, and its title comes from the first line of Eliot's poem.

About the Author

JoAnne Growney is a poet and mathematician, a former professor, a Pennsylvanian who moved south a few years ago to Washington, DC. In 2009, her chapbook *Angles of Light* was published by Finishing Line Press. For many years a collector of poems related to mathematics, Growney enjoys bringing poetry to mathematicians and mathematics to poets. She is co-editor of the anthology, *Strange Attractors: Poems of Love and Mathematics* (A K Peters, Ltd, 2008). *My Dance is Mathematics*, a collection of her own mathematical poems, was published in 2006 by Paper Kite Press. Interested in the fine arts, she has collaborated with artists in Pennsylvania, New York, and Maryland—developing poetry inspired by their work. Besides appearing in several anthologies of Pennsylvania poetry, her poems have appeared recently in *Watershed*, *Divided City*, *Poet Lore*, *Innisfree* and *Focus*. In her home neighborhood in Silver Spring, JoAnne teaches an ongoing poetry workshop at Silver Spring Drop-In Center.

To see the intersecting planes of her work, visit:
    http://joannegrowney.com,
    http://poetrywithmathematics.blogspot.com.

For information, email: japoet@msn.com.

www.ingramcontent.com/pod-product-compliance
Lightning Source LLC
Chambersburg PA
CBHW052114070526
44584CB00017B/2474